Different Shores: Love Poems From the Sea

AF624793

Lindsey Payne

BookLeaf Publishing

Different Shores: Love Poems From the Sea

Presentation by *BookLeaf Publishing*

Web: www.bookleafpub.com

E-mail: info@bookleafpub.com

ISBN: 9789357442398

First edition 2023

To all those who tried to have piece of my heart.

To the men I loved.

To the one I should have had.

Thank you for the journey.

You brought me life in all different ways.

I am forever thankful to you.

Love you in some way, always...

Lindsey

ACKNOWLEDGEMENT

The title of this book is inspired by the ending from one of my favorite books, Their Eyes Were Watching God, by Zora Neale Hurston.

"Love is lak de sea. It's uh movin' thing, but still and all, it takes its shape from de shore it meets, and it's different with every shore."

Maybe I'm Not Ready

Maybe I'm not ready

For these feelings already

The heart flutters

The faint breathing

The wishful thinking

The want and need for attention

Maybe Me, Myself, and I

Need to stick together longer

Before I include any portion of

You, Yourself, and He

Though think of how

Wonderful it could be

But here I am

Simply caught up in memories

Memories of first meetings

Talking, texting and being

Looking too deeply into a dream

Barely grasping reality

The reality that maybe

We will only have

Hopes and dreams

We will only have

Once given memories

We will only have

Distance and time

But maybe not simply

You and I

Maybe I don't want to try

Because getting simple hopes up

Is not a favorite of mine

And yes, "friends" are what we are

But there's hidden agendas

For both parties

And all this planning

Can get complicated

But why can't we be a complicated melody

Dancing slowly along

Time is truly all we have

But I'm willing to give you my time

One day

While letting these feelings

Expand and extend to your arms

But these are hopeless romantic dreams

I must get back to reality

The reality is that you and I

Keep the distance

Save the time

Fight these feelings

I'm already experiencing

And continue on each day

As if you weren't recently

Added to my life

But that would all be a lie

And I can not lie to myself

And I can not begin to lie

To you

But honestly

I feel as if these feelings

Were exposed to you

It would only make you run away

Here is the dilemma

In liking people

In liking potential mates

Maybe I'm not ready

For all this again

Maybe you aren't ready

For all this again

Maybe Me, Myself, and I

Should just continue

Without feeling for

You, Yourself, and He

But that's not how I

Want it to be

Complicated Thing

It appears as soon as I'm fallin' in

I'm fallin' out

This love is a complicated thing

Being so unsure

But I'll be okay,

I'll be fine

Hearts can't be forced right?

Hearts can't fight every night

Deciding between right and wrong

Deciding between staying or going

This love is a complicated thing

It appears as soon as I'm fallin' in

I'm fallin' out

Never seem to know which

Direction I’m heading in

This love is a complicated thing

Love, Please

Love, please forgive me

But could you turn around

And walk back out my door

I don’t want you here anymore

I know, I know

I’ve dreamed

I’ve cried

I’ve wished

I’ve hoped

I’ve prayed

All these things each longing

All for your love

Love in my heart

Love in my soul

Love, I have waited for you

And so it saddens me to say

Love, please forgive me

But go away

Love, please don’t cry

Our tears will drown the world

Love, please don’t yell

Our screams will frighten the skies

Love, please don’t be mad

Our anger will explode the earth

Yes, I am truly sorry love

Love, I am not ready for you

Oh I’ve tried and tried

Oh I’ve waited and waited

Oh I’ve cried and cried

Cried and held myself to sleep

Waiting for love to walk by

And my heart can no longer

Take it

The fight is no longer in me

The days and nights have frozen

The loneliness has reigned

Love, I’m sorry

But please go away

You can’t repair my faults

You can’t repair my mind

You can’t repair my heart

Dear Love

Love, please don't be that way

I'll be ready for you one day

These tears are starting to form

On my face

And soon I won't see

Love, please just give me time

I'll be ready

I'll be ready

Just not today

Cure

You are the drug itching

Through my veins

Knowing all the time

All the pain

Just out of rehab

And here you come again

Reminding me of a winter's past

Reminding me of a lover gone

Too fast

You are the drug I'm addicted to

Making me numb to my true feelings

Making me feel out of this world

And yet allowing me to

Crash and burn

Some know all too well the

Effect you have

Some crave you, some devour you

But they don't know you

Like I do

But they don't know the

Makings of you

You, that drug itching

Through my veins

Causing my heart to beat

A thousand pains

You are the drug that keeps

Me living

You are the drug I wanna take

To stop breathing

Ahh you give me wonderful feelings

And then leave me to wonder

I no longer cry

The tears they dried up

Too much drug

No more feelings

You are the drug that

Hides by day

And seeks by night

Sweet, sweet drug

I love you

Sweet, sweet drug

I miss you

But I'm finding peace

With sobriety

And your itch is leaving me

Don't make me fall back

Don't make me a fool

You are the drug

But I am the cure

In This Bed

As I lay in this bed

I remember you here

Sleeping sound

And probably not thinking of me

The girl who loves

But does not receive

The girl who would do for you

This girl, always a fool

This girl, being me

And now I lay

Where you once stayed

Envisioning your touch

And remembering

The words you once said

And all along

This I dread,

Dread this moment

To feel ashamed

Lost and forgotten

My love couldn’t hold you

My love couldn’t save you

My love just repelled you

Repelled you to distances

I could not reach

And as I lay here

Your words burn into my heart

And all I hold is this bed

I want to tear apart

Forgetful

Did you forget?

Forget my heart?

Forget that my heart

Has been yours since the beginning?

Did you forget to love me?

Did you forget to take care?

Did you forget what we

have shared?

I did not

I will not

Can you come back to me?

Did I hurt you?

Did you think I would forget you?

Did you think I would leave you forever?

My baby,

I’m sorry

I wouldn’t dream to

We Could Have Been

We could have been in love by now,

But egos and differences got in the way.

We could have planned

Our future by now,

But fear and doubts got in the way.

We could have everything by now,

But we are too stubborn,

We are too much for each other.

Love couldn't step in, let alone stay.

Trust walked out months ago.

Respect talked itself dead.

We could have been a lot of things,

But it just wasn't our thing.

First

I used to love you

Never thought you'd never be mine

Wished for you a thousand times

Written books in your spirit

Nightmares in your soul

I would have traveled the world

If you wanted me to

I would I have traveled for you

But greedy hands do not hold on

Selfish hearts do not bleed

And after years of playing with mine

You see

You see that my heart bled for you

My hands held on to you

My soul screamed at night for you

My spirit wrote your name in everything

Everything was about you

And while there will never be another time

I still find myself looking for you

I find you in others

Hoping one might be the better version of you

Hoping that they don't have all your colors

I think I'm doing this all wrong

You still haunt me in my dreams

I wish you would leave

I wish I never told you I'd always love you

That you'd be my forever

That you were home

I used to love you

So much I couldn't stand it

The pain and the relief

With just one look into your eyes

I used to love you

Before I learned to love me

I wish you were never mine

I'd be looking for some other to find

Web of Lies

You tried to trap me under your web of lies,

Not knowing I'd turn everything

You spun into a beautiful escape,

You tried your best to keep me

Under your spell,

Never understanding I knew your

ways of manipulation,

I am not the one you thought you could play,

I am not the one who you claimed to love,

I am the one who got away,

I am the one who took your web of lies,

And brought them to the light

To show everyone your true colors,

You thought I was an easy catch,

I just turned into your worse nightmare.

Come on and light the flame,

I'll be ready to wash you out.

Line Up

If I could line you all up

One by one

Point out each of you who

Stole my heart

Point out each of you who

Wasted my time

Point out each of you who

Told me lies

The truths would unfold

And you'd all be given

Time

Time for the all the times

You thought it was okay

To leave me stranded

To leave me unknowing

To leave me unloved

To leave me waiting

Time

Time for all the times

You claimed you wanted more

Only to follow in the footsteps

Towards the door

If I could line you all up

I would make sure you knew

All the shit you pulled

You didn't get away with it

Time is now your best friend

Time is all you have left

Time is what I'm taking back

You thought this was just a game

Until your Time ran out

Something New

You keep surprising me

Didn't think I'd like this

But here I am

Thinking about you

Thinking about the what ifs

And what am I waiting for?

Go ahead

Try something new

Create something new

Do something new

My old ways never got me far

What would be the worse to happen?

Love and Leave?

Love and Stay?

Keep the flow going

Whatever it is

I’m open

To something new

Mistakes, But No Regrets

We had many mistakes

Many regrets

Many wishes

And each and every time

Things between us couldn't be

Regardless of our feelings

You didn't want to be

I didn't want to be

Back and forth

We'd switch

And back and forth

Hurt and tears were shed

I couldn't live that way

We couldn't

Friends? No

With feelings deep inside

It wouldn't be possible

And we've proven that

It's a shame

But it's okay

I'm just fine

For sure this time

Secretly I wish,

I long for you

But it will be impossible with you

I know that much

And I can't play this tug-o-war

Between feelings

No, I can’t anymore

I’m leaving love behind

Because love never truly satisfied me

Maybe because I could

Not let it all the way in

And because I did that

I fooled myself

And because you could only hope

And because you could only imagine

Only pretend of love

I was was in love with a lie

I can’t live that way

I won’t

I don’t, not anymore

I've made my mistakes with you

As well as others

But not anymore

I've left you all behind

I will love me

And get love in return, from me

Because your love

Was never here in the first place

I realized everything

And in that, it was a lesson learned

It was building block

Therefore, I no longer regret

But just remember

So that if I get a chance

With someone else in the future

I won't repeat

I won't repeat those mistakes

I won't fall so easily

I won't give so easily

I won't do it

No, no

All The Things

I am all the things

You think I am

Because your mind won't

Allow you to see clearly

I am all the things

You think I am

Because your heart has

Grown cold

I am all the things

You think I am

Because you refuse to love

Me entirely

I am all the things

You think I am

Because you don't know me

I am all the things

You think I am

Because I simply refuse

To correct you

I am all the things

You think I am

And I am all the things

You'll never have

Tender Kisses

Blow kisses my way

Hope they land perfectly

Falling upon the tears

That shed

And creating peace

Where sorrow lives

Blow kisses my way

Hope they land perfectly

Falling upon my lips

That were formed for you

To melt our hearts into one

Blow kisses my way

Hope they land perfectly

Falling upon my forehead

To ease the anxiety

To allow my body to sleep at night

Blow kisses my way

Place kisses on me

Kiss me and all my worries away

Love, A Wanderer

I found myself in your laugh
I found myself in your smile
I found myself in your eye's reflection
I found myself in your heart
I found myself in your soul
I found myself in your dreams
And yet, I still wander
Looking for my new place to call
Home

Looking for my heart as it continues to roam

Looking for my love as I walk pass my own
reflection

Looking for my confidence to show

Looking for my reason and season to turn into
lifetime

I found myself in you

But I'm still looking for myself in me, too

Once Again

I don't know what the signs were

I don't know what I missed

I don't know if this was

Just a lesson or karma being a bitch

Timing was off

Or maybe lust confused as love

I don't know why this keeps happening

I guess I need to pay attention more

I guess I need to slow down

I guess I need to put up more boundaries

Need to stop putting hard feelings into one

Because just like that

I feel heart broken again

Like love is never on my side

Am I just selfish?

Am I undeserving?

Or was it simply the wrong time?

Before You

If I could only remember
How it felt to be loved before you
I wouldn't be searching for love in dried out souls

If I could only remember
How it felt to be loved before you
I wouldn't be searching for unyielding promises

If I could only remember
How it felt to be loved before you
I wouldn't be searching for pain to fill the void

If I could only remember
How it felt to be loved before you
I wouldn't be searching for myself in the mirror

If I could only remember
How it felt to be loved before you
I wouldn't have dared laid my eyes upon you

If I could only remember
I'd be the woman in love with self
Who knew that pain did not equate love

And I'm starting to remember…

Dear Ex Lovers

Dear Ex Lovers,

Do you still wish things were different?

Do you still wish you saw me during the times
you tried to make me different?

Do you still wish that you told me earlier of the
feelings you were hiding from me?

I still love you,

I'll always love the hearts I tried to mend

Trying to show you, you were worthy of real
love

While you stomped on my heart

Trying to show you, I was everything you
needed

While I neglected my own heart

I was a fool for you

I was intently hanging on to every word, every syllable

He said it, he will do it

He said it, he meant it

He said it, he will show me

He said it, he meant no harm

I was a fool to think my love would have changed you

Or maybe it did,

But you waited until it was gone

To see it

I still love you, yes

I still think you deserve the best, yes

I still wish for your happiness, yes

I've just learned, in all the hard ways

I love too much

I wish the love I gave you,

I gave myself

So now, it’s my turn

So now, I deserve

So now, I wish

So now, I give

All my love to me,

The one love my Ex Lovers didn’t know how to keep

Hello, It's Me

Hello, it’s me again.

I didn’t think you’d mind,
all the time we’ve spent together.
I thought I’d still be on your mind.
I didn’t think you’d forget me so fast.
Is my time gone from the hour glass?

Hey, it’s me again.
Remember how I used to hold your hand?
Remember the long kisses that would
make you lose your fight to stand?
Remember the long nights of talking?
Hearing your voice slowly fade,
as you tried to fight sleeping.

Yo, it’s me again.
Did you forget me?
I thought I meant the world to you?
I know I left, but I thought you knew,
I’d be back for you.
I tried to be cool,
Not front on missing you.
Didn’t you miss me?
You must be a fool.

What's up, it's me again.
You remember that girl still?
Nah, she wasn't for me.
I told you, I just need you.
Remember our first date?
I told you I'd marry you.
You know I was serious.
I didn't think you'd move on.
Seriously, just c'mon.

Sorry, it's me again.
I know I did you wrong.
But you were always the one.
But you were different.
But you were supposed to wait.
I'm sorry, its so late.
I'm sorry, can we try again?
I'm sorry....

Hello?
click

Hello?
delete

Hello?
block

Rebirth Self-Love

I gave my heart another chance

Took her by surprise

Gave her all I ever had to give

Took back all the lies

Took back all the shame

Took back all the doubts

Begged for forgiveness

And showed up not only with words

But with my actions

I promised to listen within

I promised to hold on

I promised our breaks would mend

I gave my heart another chance

She loved me every step of the way

She loved me for all that I was

She loved me for all I was never meant to be

I gave my heart another chance

She held me and said don't worry

She told me I will wipe your tears

She told me she forgave me

I am back home where I belong

I am home where my heart is

I am home with me

She's the best love I could have ever asked for

She's me

The One

I’ve spent too much time over the years

Trying to prove my worth

To men, to boys

Who claimed that I was The One

I am The One

The One constantly losing

Because these men, these boys

Don’t know how to love me

I am The One

The One constantly fighting myself

To prove I can wait

For them to come back

When they are ready

I am The One

The One constantly questioning my

definition of who I am

Because I've let them manipulate me

Into thinking I need them for validation

I am The One

The One constantly loving

And giving more of me than I will ever

receive of them

Because that's what unconditional love is

But they love with conditions

Conditions I can no longer meet

I am The One

This is true

The One they will forever compare others to

I am The One

The One respecting myself and leaving

you

www.ingramcontent.com/pod-product-compliance
Lightning Source LLC
Chambersburg PA
CBHW051736130826
49812CB00033B/886

* 9 7 8 9 3 5 7 4 4 2 3 9 8 *